I0529564

My Little Red Book

The CheezeBoy

Copyright © 2022 by The CheezeBoy

Paperback: 978-1-959224-34-1
eBook: 978-1-959224-35-8
Library of Congress Control Number: 2022923160

All rights reserved. No part of this publication may be
reproduced, distributed, or transmitted in any form or
by any electronic or mechanical means, without the prior
written permission of the publisher, except in the case of brief
quotations embodied in critical reviews and certain other
noncommercial uses permitted by copyright law.

Ordering Information:

Prime Seven Media
518 Landmann St.
Tomah City, WI 54660

Printed in the United States of America

TABLE OF CONTENTS

PART 1

HELL AND BACK 03/10/2014 07:21........................ 2

WHAT A WEEKEND I'VE HAD

05/10/2014 17:40 3

IT'S EARLY DECEMBER

09/12/2014 22:30 4

+ WE NEED GOOD RELIGION +

23/01/2015.. 5

25/02/2015 6

WORKING NIGHTS

23/02/2015 15:00 7

IS ANYBODY CALLING ME?

09/03/2015 15:10... 8

HUMAN NATURE

20/03/2015 21:45... 9

MYTHS AND LEGENDS

26/03/2015 23:00 10

STILL AT THE CROSSROADS

01/04/2015 22:15.. 11

ROCKING ALL OVER THE PLACE

10/04/2015 21:26.. 12

IT'S APRIL RAINING

29/04/2015 07:46 16

SITTIN' AT DOBBYN'S

30/04/2015 17

I'M SO SAD

18/05/2015 21:23 18

NO, NO, NO

23/05/2015 22:53.. 19

IT'S A GUINEA PIG DAY

24/05/2015 22:17 20

R THEY ?

01/04/2015 20:53 21

P . N . E . ROAR

24/05/2015 22:33 22

PAY - RISE 23

PAPA'S ON THE BEACH

24/05/2015 15:06 24

SHREDDING

24/05/2015 21:08..25

GHOSTS

27/05/2015 0:15 26

GIVE IT A GO

27/05/2015 22:14 27

PART 2

GRANTHAM WEEKENDER
01/06/2015 16:30......................................30

+ ANOTHER KENNEDY DEAD +
02/06/2015 32

NO SMILERS AT ALTON TOWERS
02/06/2015 33

BLATTER'S NOT GONE 02/06/2015
(ADDED LAST LINES: BLATTER'S
FINALLY GONE 16/03/2016 0:22) 34

OH WHAT A DAY
03/06/2015 15:28 35

STEPH AND ME...36

SUNDOWN BLUES
15/06/2015 22:53......................................37

ON THE SMOKESTREAM
15/06/2015 23:12..38

NO - ONE WON . NO - ONE HAD FUN
06/07/2015 23:51.......................................39

IMPORTIN' BLUES
29/07/2015 0:19.......................................40

GIG LIFE
29/07/2015 22:59......................................41

+ CILLA BLACK +
08/08/2015 17:58.......................................43

CIRCLE CLINIC
12/10/2015 18:10 44

IN THE NEWSERS
13/08/2015 14:28..45

SPOOKS AND ZOMBIES.
NIGHTMARES AND DREAMS
18/08/2015 22:22..46

I'M GONNA WONDER.
IS THAT THUNDER ?
20/08/2015 0:10..47

STILL IMPORTIN'
20/08/2015 22:22 48

COLWICK LIFE
21/08/2015 16:00..49

I'M IN LOVE
27/08/MMXV 16:02..50

CHEEZETUNEZ THRILL
30/08/MMXV 15:29 51

BOWLING FUNDAY,
BANK HOLIDAY MONDAY
01/09/MMXV 0:46..53

IT'S BEEN NON - STOP
17/09/2015 21:42 54

WHAT DID I WRITE T'OTHER NITE ?
19/09/2015 21:01...55

MY LITTLE 'UN
20/09/2015 20:13 56

I'M A BELIEVER
28/09/2015 22:27 57

MOON + STARS
01/10/2015 22:34... 58

ON THE WINDS OF CHANGE
 02/10/2015 59

POETRY DAY
08/10/2015 19:30...60

THE THRILL HAS GONE
17/10/2015 21:41 61

FAMILY HALLOWEEN
03/11/2015 62

DREAMS, SCREAMS, BODY CREAMS
16/11/2015 15:15...63

IS IT THE END OF US ?
19/11/2015 14:41 64

GIG NIGHTS
26/11/2015 22:41 65

WEATHER'S BEEN COLD, WET AND GREY
28/11/2015 18:13...66

MILLIEKIN BLUES
28/11/2015 20:15 67

STRONGBOWADE
28/11/2015 20:53...68

IN THE LAND OF NEVER
29/11/2015 15:12 69

THE WIND IS HOWLING.
THE WIND IS GROWLING
29/11/2015 18:51 70

THE STARS ARE OUT
04/12/2105 0:36.. 72

BOO HOO HOO
04/12/2015 22:27 73

ICE ROAD TRUCKIN'
 08/12/2015 0:36.. 74

+ LEE HARVEY +
08/12/2015 12:01.. 75

SUNNY WEDNESDAY
09/12/2015 12:09 76

NUMBERS, NUMBERS
10/12/2015 16:34... 77

IT'S DARK AND GLOOMY. IS ANYBODY
COMING FOR ME?
10/12/2015 17:01 78

MY LITTLE
RED BOOK 10/12/2015 20:00.................................... 80

PART 1

WORDS of CheezeDom
POEMS and RANTS

WARNING! Contains some strong
and offensive language!

HELL AND BACK
03/10/2014 07:21

I've been to hell and back. I've been through
high water. I've been through low water. I've
been through deep water. I've been through
dark water. I've nearly been to the slaughter.
I've lost a daughter, little A. I've gained another
beautiful daughter, little L. She's the best.
Me and her mummy have been Blessed by GOD.
Oh my GOD! What went wrong? The last 7 years
have done me wrong. I'd Love to get some ding-
dong. I've been to hell and back. I've been on a trip.
I nearly flipped. Getting better now. I'm at the
end of the trip. I'm nearly back. I'm nearly back. I
see the end. GOD is my friend. I Love You All.
I'm nearly back. I'm nearly back.
From hell and back. From hell and back.
From hell and back.

WHAT A WEEKEND I'VE HAD
05/10/2014 17:40

What a weekend I've had. Seeing my Emily
made me glad to be her dad. We've had lots of
fun. We've been to Goose Fair. We've been to
Stonebridge City Farm. Where sheep, goats
and cows eat out of the hands, on your arms.
Goose Fair was great. Had loads of fun. Been on
slides and helter skelters with my little 1. What
a weekend I've had. It's been happy and glad.
Not boring and sad.
What a weekend I've had. What a weekend I've had.
What a weekend I've had.
What a great weekend I've had.

IT'S EARLY DECEMBER 09/12/2014 22:30

It's early December. Do you remember? Santa
comes soon, past the Moon, over the Poles,
through the Trees. On his Sleigh and Reindeer,
coming to please thee. What will I get?
Did Santa forget? Have I been a good boy, or
a bad boy? I hope Santa will bring everybody
joy. Is it a bike? Is it a mike? Is it a toy?
To bring great joy. It's Christmas time. It's
nursery rhyme. It's CheezeBoy rhyme.
It's Christmas time. Will you be fine?
Everybody singing Christmas rhymes. Everybody
singing Christmas carols. Everyone drinking
heated Mulled Wine. It's Christmas time.
It's Christmas time soon, past the Moon.
It's early December. Do you remember? It's
early December. Do you remember?

+ WE NEED GOOD RELIGION + 23/01/2015

+ It's snowed. It's rained. It's sunned. It's been cold. It's been warm. It's nearly February. I aint been re-born. For Dad and Addison. We did mourn. God look after them both. Could you please + Help the World. Help the Unease. The Evil Religion. The Terrorist Disease. The Good Religion has to be released and give the Evil Religion a mighty squeeze. God could you please Help the World. The Terrorist disease. Is it worth saving? This Human Race? Do wonders never cease? We need Good Religion to Cure the Disease. We need Good Religion. We need Good Religion. We need Good Religion to Cure the Disease. We need Good Religion. We need Good Religion. We need Good Religion. Amen. +

25/02/2015

Had a gud nite. No frite. Great delite. Working with Monika. A Beautiful Polish delite. Did over 200k, horay, horay. I did myself proud. Had a Hard Day's Nite, with Polish Delite. Gud morning. Gudbye. Gudnite.

WORKING NIGHTS
23/02/2015 15:00

1 more spliff before the News and Top
Gear. Working all night. Holy shite. So
no more beer and no more gear.
Then it's all hunky dorey, jackanory, what's the
story, morning glory. 1 more spliff before the
News and Top Gear. Working all night. Holy
shite. Not to fear. There'll be no more beer, and
they'll be no more cheer. 1 more spliff before
the News and Top Gear. Working all night.
Holy shite.
Then it's all hunky dorey, jackanory, what's the
story, morning glory. 1 more spliff before the
News and Top Gear. Working nights. Holy shite.
Everything's hunky dorey, jackanory, what's the
story, morning glory. Everything's hunky dorey,
jackanory, what's the story, morning glory.
Working nights. Holy shite.
Goodbye folks. I'm working nights.
Everything's hunky dorey, jackanory,
what's the story, morning glory.
Working nights. Working nights.
Working nights. Holy shite.

IS ANYBODY CALLING ME? 09/03/2015 15:10

Is anybody calling me? Is anybody calling me?
Is anybody calling me? When will I see the
Queen Bee? I'm happy about the tricky trees.
Is anybody calling me? Is anybody calling
me? Is anybody calling me? It's horrible being
lonely. When will I see the Queen Bee?
I'm happy about the tricky trees.
When will I get some please?
Is anybody calling me? Is anybody calling me?
Is anybody calling me? Is anybody calling me?
Is anybody calling me? Is anybody calling me?
Where is the Queen Bee?
Is anybody calling me? Is anybody
calling me? Is anybody calling me?

HUMAN NATURE
20/03/2015 21:45

Human Nature. It's got some Strange and Awful Features. We're Strange Creatures. We've gots lots of Good and lots of Bad. Even the Happiest Times can be Sad. Human Nature. Human Nature. We're Strange Creatures. With lots of Features. With Magic and Madness. With Joyous and Sadness. With Tears of Joy and Tears of Pain. We're Insane in the Membrane. Human Nature. Human Nature. We're Strange Creatures. With lots of Features. There's Amazement. There's Abandonment. There's Crazyment. Human Nature. Human Nature. There's Joy and Pain. Insane in the Membrane. There's Happiness and Sadness. There's Victory and Defeat. There's War and Peace. There's lots of Disease. There's lots of Cure. There's lots of Us, so We Need More. It's Human Nature Knocking at Your Door. It's Human Nature. It's Human Nature. It's Human Nature Knocking at Your Door. We Want Peace. We Don't Want War. It's Human Nature. It's Human Nature. It's Human Nature.

MYTHS AND LEGENDS 26/03/2015 23:00

I think all these Myths and Legends
are Really Real. World's Unsticking.
Poltergeists are Knocking. Cupboards are
Opening. Doors are Swinging. Orbs are
Flying. Werewolves are Growling.
Myths and Legends. Myths and Legends.
Are They Here? Are They There? Are They
Already Everywhere? Need We Be Cautious? Need
We Fear? Are Myths and Legends Really Here?
Myths and Legends. Myths and Legends.
Are Vampires Creeping Around The Night?
Bringing Fear. Bringing Fright. Myths and
Legends, Thrilling The Night. Bringing Fear.
Bringing Delight. Myths and
Legends. Myths and Legends.
Are They Real? How Do You Feel?
Are They Real? Are They Real?
Myths and Legends. Myths and Legends…?

STILL AT THE CROSSROADS 01/04/2015 22:15

Getting the hang of this Guitar. Is it real? Will my wounds start to heal? Will my dreams start to feel like they may possibly become real? Still at the crossroads. Still trying to hear. I play better than ever now, Holy Cow. I'm getting words muddled. I'm splashing in muddy puddles. This writing is fun. The dream has begun. I love my Guitar's. Got a New Amp. Marshall of course. Still at the crossroads. Still full of fear. The dream has begun. The dream maybe here. Still at the crossroads. Still don't know what direction to go. Will I ever make it onto the Radio? Still at the crossroads. Still at the crossroads. Still at the crossroads.

ROCKING ALL OVER THE PLACE 10/04/2015 21:26

With Lynott on Bass. McCartney's Wings start to race. Rocking all over the place. That would be ace. Hendrix on Guitar. Beatles afar. Moon and Baker on the Drums. Eminem grabbing his plums. Oh the door is ajar. Who's at the bar? Jones and Barrett with Jasper Carrott. Chilling it down with Buddy Holly and B I G. Chilling it down without a frown. With Harrison and Springfield wearing Crown's. Now back to the Gig after my Funny Cigs.

Who's playing now? Wow, Wow, Wow. Kinks are there. So are The Doors. And over there, without scare. it's Nirvana, Johnson and Waters. Watch your Daughters. it's Queen too and The Who. The Floyd, The Stones, The Roses. The Guns are having fun. Rocking all over the place.

Cast are having a blast. There's Ocean Colour Scene, Lenny Kravitz, The Verve, Sash, Pink, Beach Boys, Kate Bush, Yardbirds, Kylie, Madonna, Fun Lovin' Criminals, Katy Perry, Feeder, Fratellis, Iron

Maiden and Keane. Shed Seven, Franz Ferdinand, Blur, Jamiroquai and Gomez. Is it Heaven? Is it Heaven? Is it Cloud 9? Will this be the only time? I love to rhyme. I feel fine.

Just in time for Earth, Wind and Fire, with Melvin Van Peebles, Isaac Hayes and Metallica. It can't be! Seriously? It is! It's Jackson, Presley and Orbison. This will be awesome. Oh Wow, Wow, Wow. And over there. I can't believe my stare. It's Brown, White, Green, Mayfield, Diamond and Gaye, jamming away. What a happy day. I'm chilling the groove. I don't want to move. Rocking all over the place. Oh my word! I just heard. Joy Division and Troggs, to join The Jam. I better start running. Everybody's coming. This is the Gig. This is the Gig.

Cream are here, So are Muse. Oasis too, The Stereophonics 3, Portishead, Radiohead and Prodigy. Kaisers and Kasabian, The Peppers are Red Hot. Crouch doing the Robot. Rocking all over the place. This Gig is ace. My heart starts to race. I don't believe it! I don't believe it!

Garbage are there. Pulp are there. Oh how shall I style the last of my hair? U2 are giving me a stare, over there. Rocking all over the place. Marley is chilling. Everyone's winning. Rocking all over the place. Where's my Lynx? It's INXS. Trouble brewing. Is security coming? It's Mr T and the other A-Team 3. Not to worry. Job done. Everyone safe. Everyone won.

I saw Bon Jovi, T-Rex, Led Zepp, Van Morrison, Meatloaf, The Velvets, Nico and R.E.M., over there then. Dawson, Morecambe and Wise having fun. With Hale and Pace, Smith and Jones, Lee Evans, Mrs Brown, Enfield and Whitehouse, chuckling at the moon. Billy Fury, Gene Pitney, Russell Watson, Eva Cassidy, The 3 Tenors, Then it's Billie Holiday, Louis Armstrong, Nina Simone, Killers, Snow Patrol, Fugees, Winehouse, Withers, Wonder, Manics, Blondie, Alanis, Take That, Bryan Adams, Sinatra, Jerry Lee Lewis, Little Richard, Tina Turner, Jefferson Airplane, Janis Joplin and Santana. More fun for everyone! Then Aerosmith, Aretha, Smiths, Run DMC, Johnny Cash and the Bee Gees. I've got trembling knees.

The Animals, David McWilliams, Byrds, Bob Dylan, Joe Cocker, TLC, Charlatans, Coldplay, Cranberries, Arctic Monkeys, David Bowie, Deep Purple, Motorhead, Black Sabbath, Happy Mondays, Fleetwood Mac, Elton John, ZZ Top, ELO, Springsteen, Simon and Garfunkel, Genesis, Roxy Music, ELP, Prince, Eurythmics, Madness, Specials, UB40, Simply Red, Steppenwolf, AC/DC, Boyzone,

Spice Girls, Alice Cooper, BB King, A-Ha, Lynyrd Skynrd, Duran Duran, Free, Police, Bad Company, and the Quo. Before the end of the show. What a day.

Everyone home safe. Everyone had fun. Everyone won. Rocking all over the place. Rocking all over the place. Rocking all over the place. I need to sit down for a Bit. Hit after Hit after Hit. That was it! This is it!

IT'S APRIL RAINING
29/04/2015 07:46

It's April raining. Green room is spinning. Am I losing? Am I winning? It's April raining. Birds still singing. Guinea Pigs are squeaking. Cats are meowing. Dogs are barking. Hounds are howling.

It's April raining. It's April raining.

May aint far away. Bank Holiday soon. Bright red Moon. It's April raining. Green room is spinning. Am I losing? Am I winning? Sore crack is back. Sore back is back. Pilates Cure. Need I say more?

It's April raining. It's April raining.

Green room is spinning. My head is too. I don't know what to do?

Too-Da-Loo.

It's April raining. It's April raining. It's April raining.

SITTIN' AT DOBBYN'S 30/04/2015

Sittin' at Dobbyn's lookin' at the sky. Seein'
Birds flyin', flyin' high. Floatin' on the wind,
floatin' by. **Grey**-white clouds and blue sky.
Seein' Birds flyin', flyin' high. Floatin'
on the wind, floatin' by.
Sittin' at Dobbyn's lookin' at the sky. The World is
big. The World is high. Sittin' at Dobbyn's lookin'
at the sky. **Grey**-white clouds and blue sky.
I'm sittin' at Dobbyn's. I'm sittin' at
Dobbyn's. I'm sittin' at Dobbyn's.

I'M SO SAD
18/05/2015 21:23

I'm so sad. I'm so sad. I'm sad, I'm sad, I'm sad. I'm
so mad. I'm so mad. I'm mad, I'm mad, I'm mad. I'm
not glad. I'm not glad. I'm sad, I'm sad, I'm sad.
I'm not bad. I'm not bad. I'm good, I'm good,
I'm good. Am I mad? Am I mad? I'm mad,
I'm mad, I'm mad. Am I lost? Am I lost?
I'm lost, I'm lost, I'm lost. I'm not found. I'm
not found. I'm lost, I'm lost, I'm lost.
At what cost? At what cost? I'm lost, I'm lost,
I'm lost. I'm not dead. I'm not dead. I've got a
muddled head. I'm in bed. I'm in bed. I'm sad,
I'm sad, I'm sad. What went wrong? What
went wrong? I'm lost, I'm lost, I'm lost.
I'm so sad. I'm so sad. I'm sad, I'm sad, I'm sad.
Goodbye folks. Goodbye folks.
I'm sad, I'm sad, I'm sad.

NO, NO, NO
23/05/2015 22:53

No, No, No, let me go. I've had enough. I wanna
go home. Watching Muse all alone. I wish E.T.
would phone a girl for me and send her to my home.
Where we can have some fun and I won't be alone.
No, No, No, let me go. I wanna go home. I don't
wanna be alone. No, No, No, let me go. Leave
me alone. Take me home. I've had enough. I've
had enough. Take me home. Leave me alone.
No, No, No, let me go. Leave me alone. I
wanna go home. That's what I say. No wonder
I don't get a lay. hand-job time. I'll be fine.
No, No, No, let me go. Leave me alone.
I like to moan. It's how I am.
I don't have a plan.
No, No, No, let me go. Leave me alone. I
wanna go home. No, No, No, let me go.
Leave me alone. I wanna go home.
No, No, No, let me go.
No, No, No, I'm gonna go. I've had
enough. I wanna go home.
No, No, No, let me go. Leave me
alone. I'm going home.
No, No, No, let me go. No, No, No.
No, No, No, I gotta go.

IT'S A GUINEA PIG DAY 24/05/2015 22:17

What is this feeling? I'm climbing the ceiling. I'm crawling the walls. Closing the doors. What is this feeling? My mind is reeling. Where's the pit-stop? How long have I got? I almost forgot! What is this feeling? What have I done? Have I jumped the gun? What is this feeling? A music Shop. What I forgot! What do I play?

It's a Guinea Pig Day. What is this feeling? I'm climbing the ceiling. I'm crawling the walls. Opening the doors. It's a Guinea Pig Day. What do you say? It's a wonderful feeling. Its a Guinea Pig Day. What do you say? It's a Guinea pig Day. What is this feeling? It's a Guinea Pig Day. What is this feeling? I'm going away. It's a Guinea Pig Day. Happy Guinea Pig Bank Holiday.

R THEY ?
01/04/2015 20:53

Maybe they R. I'm strumming Guitar. Writing sum words. Who is there? R They real? R spooks in the room? Witch on her broom. Wolves on the Moon. My Green Room. Roger and out. Creeping about. R They here? R They everywhere? R They strumming Guitar? Ta-Ra.

P . N . E . ROAR
24/05/2015 22:33

Did U go to Wembley 4 the P.N.E. Roar? Garners
Goal, was a wonder to behold. Happy Bank Holiday.
LilyWhites through the Championship Door. C
U next season. P.N.E. Roar. Get in my son.
Has the end to Ana's Chicken Pox
begun? I Love U All. P.N.E. Roar.
L.O.L.! Roger and out.

PAY - RISE

Pay-Rise! What Pay-Rise? The
Boxes are Stacked Against Us!
Destroy the Trees! Bring the World to it's Knees!
Consume the Oil! We have Trouble and Toil!
Leak all the Gas! What Will Power Us? Pay-Rise!
What Pay-Rise? The Boxes are Stacked Against
Us! No New Money, Ended Up Coming to thee.
Pay-Rise! What's A Pay- Rise? Bluekins Greed
Got to Them! So No Pay-Rise, Yet Again!

PAPA'S ON THE BEACH 24/05/2015 15:06

Papa's on the beach gettin' a Suntan. He doesn't know he's at Risk from Skin Cancer. He's a High Skin Cancer Risk. He should just put on Suncream. Put on Suncream. Papa can then enjoy the Sunshine and live the dream.
Papa's on the beach gettin' a Suntan.
He's not wearin' Suncream.
He's a Man. High Skin Cancer Risk for a Suntan.
Papa put on Suncream. Livin' the dream. Papa put on Suncream. Livin' the dream. Papa's just put on some Suncream. Livin' the dream.
Papa's on the beach gettin' a Suntan.
He's Now Wearin' Suncream.
He's a Man. Sunnin' himself. Sunnin' himself. Sunnin' himself.
Livin' the dream. Wearin' Suncream.
Papa's on the beach. Papa's on the beach.

SHREDDING
24/05/2015 21:08

Where am I? Why am I here? I need a strongbow cider. Am I here? Am I there? Am I already everywhere? I just don't know! I just don't know! Been Shredding the news. Shredding the abuse. Shredding the spam. Shredding the junk. Dunking the gunk. Shredding the news. Shredding the views. Shredding the letters, With my Shredder. Shredding the pain. Shredding the balloons. Drinking a strongbow cider. Had a tooth removed. Blood and pain. Pain in the brain. The wisdow has gone, but only 1 of them. Still got 3 attached to me. Well tricky trees did'nt please. Always next Season? I need a strongbow cider. Where am I? Why am I here? I need a strongbow cider. Am I here? Am I there? Am I already everywhere? Shredding away most of the day. Shredding with my Shredder. Enjoyed it too. Been Shredding away. Wahey!

GHOSTS
27/05/2015 0:15

Watchin' a hauntin'. Ghosts in my head. Darkenin'
my dreams, just before bed. Spookin' myself.
Ghosts in my head. Watchin' a hauntin'. I love my
Ghosts. I love my Ghosts. Had things happen to
me, that I cannot explain. Ghosts are Real. Ghosts
are Real. There's things out there, scientists can't
explain. Ghosts in my head. Ghosts in your brain.
There's things out there, no-one can explain.

Ghosts in your head. Ghosts in my brain.
Paranormal things testin' the brain. Darkenin' our
dreams, just before bed. Ghosts in our head, just
before bed. Ghosts on the brain, drivin' me insane.
Ghosts in my head, just before bed. Nightmares
are here, just had a beer. Ghosts in my head, just
before bed. Ghosts in our heads, just before bed.

GIVE IT A GO
27/05/2015 22:14

Well I'm at the end of *My Little Red Book, Part 1*. To be honest it didn't take too long. I'm full of rhyme. I'm full of song. *Part 2* won't be long. I'm gonna try to do it right. Change my plight. Give it a go. Give it a fight. Give it delight. Give it a go. Do it right. Don't do it wrong. Because it's taking too long, to right the wrong. I'm full of rhyme. I'm full of song. It's taking ages to right the wrong. Well who's to blame? Was it what's her name? I dunno. I dunno. I'm full of ryme. Is it this time? I'm full of song. *Part 2* won't be long. Give it a go. Give it a go. *Part 1*'s over. Roger and out. I'm full of rhyme. I'm full of song.

Part 2 won't be long.

Give it a go. Give it a go. Give it a go. Give it a go. Change your plight. Give it a go. Maybe it works? I dunno. Give it a go.

THIS IS THE END OF MY LITTLE
RED BOOK : PART 1 ...
ALSO AVAILABLE : *MY LITTLE*
BLUE BOOK (2006 - 2014)

pArt 2

WORDS of CheezeDom
POEMS and RANTS

**WARNING! Contains some strong
and offensive language!**

GRANTHAM WEEKENDER 01/06/2015 16:30

Grantham Weekender for a bloke called Chris.
At Helens House, which is like a Tardis.
Loved it all. Glad I answered the call.
Grantham Weekender for a bloke
called Chris. Lots of Fancy dress.
Lots of people pissed. Loved it all.
Glad I answered the call.
Lots of Karaoke. Lots of bliss.
Grantham Weekender for a bloke called Chris.
At Helens House. He dressed like Queen, Freddie
style. Great look. You could write a book. I was
a 1970's BeerBottle. You should see the photos.
I partied without fear. Gangsters and Molls.
CowGirls tole. Steph Red Riding Hood made me
feel good. What a beautiful MILF, without the filth.
Dueting all night gave me great delight. 3 Little
Kittens. Supermans Mittens. General about.
Grantham Weekender for a bloke called Chris.
At Helens House. Girl Ghost in the Cellar,

gave me a fright. It chilled me to the bone.
The Girl Ghost walked straight through
me. I could feel her, I could smell her, but I
couldn't see her! Attic bed, ached my legs.
Steph Red Riding Hood made me feel good.
Grantham Weekender for a bloke called Chris. Gave
everyone delight. Gave everyone bliss. Amazing
night. Girl ghost in the Cellar, gave me a fright.
The Garden was the best. The SmokeStream was
blessed. Sitting there forgetting the mess. Watching
the Stream, thinking the dream. Chilling it down.
Pizza Clown (get **blonde** moments sometimes).
Steph Red Riding Hood made me feel good.
Grantham Weekender for a bloke called
Chris. Amazing time. amazing bliss. It
made me feel tall. ThankYou all.
Grantham Weekender. At Helens House.
At Helens House. At Helens House.

+ ANOTHER KENNEDY DEAD + 02/06/2015

+ Another Kennedy dead. But not shot in the head. He drank lots of shots. So it was alcohol instead. Really liked him. Voted for him once. I liked him a lot. Charles Kennedy R.I.P. You rest peacefully. Another Kennedy dead. +

NO SMILERS AT ALTON TOWERS 02/06/2015

No smilers at Alton towers. The staff forgot to
stop the carriage. There'll be some poor people
claiming for damages. No smilers at Alton Towers.
A Roller-Coaster ride, that ended in fright.
Not delight. Them poor people. Who really,
nearly died. No smilers at Alton Towers.

BLATTER'S NOT GONE 02/06/2015 (ADDED LAST LINES: BLATTER'S FINALLY GONE 16/03/2016 0:22)

So Blatter's not gone. They done FIFA wrong.
Accepting bribes to help decide. At least 8 more.
Back-Hander by the door. Thanks very much.
So Blatter's not gone. They done FIFA wrong.
Blatter's finally gone. The New Era
begun. The Old Era did FIFA wrong.

OH WHAT A DAY
03/06/2015 15:28

Oh what a day. Compressor nearly on it's way out. Gave the Engineer a shout. What a week. I changed my speak. Oh what a day. Played some stuff. It still sounds rough. Will I ever get there? Does anybody care? I don't know? Lets have a go. Oh what a day.

The day's go away and nothing's changed. What has been arranged? Nothing yet. People forget Nowhere Men. Does anybody care? Will I ever get there? Oh what a day. Life's like a play. Nowhere Men never forget. Nowhere Men always get upset. Nowhere Men always regret. Nowhere Men, go Nowhere fast. Will you be remembered? Are you 1 of the few? Will you be the Nowhere Man, that people remember you? Oh what a day. Oh what a day. Oh what a day.

Happy Birthday Stuart. Owls
and Trees, didn't please.
Southend, Preston and Norwich
up. In the Play-Off teacup.
England now to cheer up the day. Hope you
have a very good day. Happy Birthday.

STEPH AND ME

STEPH and Me had great CHEMISTRY. I like that GIRL. We JAMMED a lot. I like that GIRL. NATIONAL ANTHEMS now to SING. WHAT IF I'D given her MY NUMBER? Would SHE have given ME a RING? What would have happened? I didn't though. I simply FORGOT!

STEPH and ME had great CHEMISTRY. You never know... LIFE IS A MYSTERY...? Had a SURPRISE this morning... I saw MY LUCY with her MUM, going to the SHOP. I LOVE our LITTLE 1. SHE brings great FUN. GOODBYE for NOW. The MATCH has begun.

SUNDOWN BLUES
15/06/2015 22:53

Just been playing the sundown blues. Some
was good. Some I can't use. Just been playing
the sundown blues. It helped me relax. It
helped my brain choose, to turn off for a bit.
Just been playing the sundown blues.
It helped my soul muse.
Manic Monday. Manic Sunday. Monday was
fun day. Sunday was a good day. A Lucy day.
A Guinea Pig day. Manic Monday was a good
day, with call-off's to do. Lots of little runs.
But why so few? Going to customers.
But for who?
Just been playing the sundown blues. Just
been playing the sundown blues. Just
been writing the sundown blues.

ON THE SMOKESTREAM 15/06/2015 23:12

When I was on the SmokeStream, I was living the
dream. Just for 1 night. On the SmokeStream, living
the dream. Just for 1 night. What a delight. Lots of
joy. Lots of delight. Best 1 ever in the never, never.
Karaoke Cheeze spreading the disease
of good love. A hayfever sneeze.
On the SmokeStream, living the dream. Just
for 1 night. Gave it my all. Stood real tall.
Everyone liked me. I gave them all a taste of
Cheeze. Giving his all, standing tall, having a
ball. Like memories of Old, memories of New.
I was Cool that night. BeerBottle Plight?
Gave a great memory on the
SmokeStream, living the dream.
On the SmokeStream. On the
SmokeStream. On the SmokeStream.
On the SmokeStream.

NO - ONE WON .
NO - ONE HAD FUN
06/07/2015 23:51

Is it Nirvana? Is it Instant Karma?
Teen Spirit? Come as You are?
Wish I had a Car. Fiddling with a Bra. Having
some Fun. No-One has Won. No-One had Fun.
No-One has Won. No-One had Fun. No-One has
Won. Is it Nirvana? Is it Instant Karma? Teen
Spirit? Get me a Double? Careful there. Looks like
trouble. If it goes wrong. There'll be lots of rubble.
Is it Nirvana. Is it Instant Karma? Where is
the Fun? Did anyone Won? Where is the Fun?
Who Won? Who had the Fun? Was it the
Devil? Was it God? Who was the Creator?
Who's the Boss? Who had the Fun? Who's
holding the Smoking Gun? Is it Nirvana? Is it
Instant Karma? No-One Won. No-One had Fun.
That's all I Remember? Return to Sender.
No-One Won. No-One had Fun. No-One Won. No-
One had Fun. No- One Won. No-One had Fun.

IMPORTIN' BLUES
29/07/2015 0:19

Layin' an' chillin'. Importin' some tunes. Listenin'
to some music. Importin' some tunes. got tonnes of
albums. Got all sorts of tunes. Importin' them to
my I Tunes. Chillin' the blues. I'm gettin' there. I
Forgot my care. Importin' tunes. Gettin' the blues.
This is a game I win an' a game I
don't lose. Layin' an' chillin'.
Importin' some tunes. Listenin' to some
music. Importin' some tunes.
I'm gettin' there. I lost my care. Layin' an'
chillin'. Importin' some tunes. Listenin'
to some music. Importin' some tunes.
This time I'm winnin'. This time I'm winnin'.
Layin' an' chillin'. This time I'm winnin'. Layin' an'
chillin'. Layin' an' chillin'. Importin' some tunes.
I've got importin' blues. I've got importin'
blues. I've got importin' blues.
I've just been writin' an' importin' blues.

GIG LIFE
29/07/2015 22:59

I've seen Kasabian from Leicester, 3 times a
pleasure. Seen Jamiroquai play, a long time
away. Oasis too. Man City blue. Seen Feeder, 3
times a pleasure. Seen Charlatans twice. They
rolled the dice. Public Enemy soon. Over the
Moon. Got Prodigy too, for number 2.
Then early next year. Fun Lovin' Criminals to
cheer. Happy Mondays soon. Over the Moon.
Seen Rolling Stones twice. They rolled the
tumbling dice. Cast were Heavenly. Sitting near
My Old Enemy J.A., all of the day. No words
said. Just tears and fears and sunburn instead.
Sterophonics were Heavenly. The most amazing
Melody. Kaiser Chiefs were great. I Predict
a Riot at the gate. Blondie were brill.
Scissor sisters thrill. Dizee Rascal was Cool.
Don't be a fool. Ocean Colour Scene were great,
but we were late through the gate and missed half
the show. So we ended up with riverboat woe.
Seen Miss Saigon once. My only show. It was
really amazing and awesome though. My most

gigs were, the Bootleg Beatles shows. Mind Blowing everytime. Nearest I'll ever get to the real Beatles in my life. I wasn't born then. John, George, Paul and Ringo. Bless Them. There'll never be another band like them again.

That's all my gig life so far. I hope there are more to come. Itchy Plums. Goodbye for now. Goodbye. Got the Charlatans again.

Amen.

+ CILLA BLACK +
08/08/2015 17:58

+++ Cilla Black. Cilla White. She was a bright
light. Brought lots of delight. Now her soul
is on a Heavenly roll to the Pearly Gates.
She truly was a great. God Bless you
Cilla. Enjoy the Heavenly flight Ta-Ra
Cilla. Goodbye. Goodnight. +++

CIRCLE CLINIC
12/10/2015 18:10

Been to the Circle Clinic today. I managed to find my way. Torn my Arse. What a farce. Lots of Sexy Nurses with Nice Arse's. Been to the Clinic today. I managed to find my way. Torn my Arse. But I'm not gay. Torn my Arse some other way. It hurts like hell, when my bowel empties my muck sometimes. Back there in 2 months time. Here I come. Got blood coming out my bum. Been to the Circle Clinic today. I found my way. Been to the Circle. Been to the Clinic. Been to the Circle. Been to the Clinic. Been to the Circle Clinic today.

IN THE NEWSERS
13/08/2015 14:28

Newsers, Losers, Beggars, Chooses. Winners,
Losers, Beggars, Chooses. Newsers, Losers,
Beggars, Choosers. What's it about?
Who do I shout? Is it a He? Is it
a She? What's it about?
Newsers, Losers, Beggars, choosers. Winners,
Losers, Beggars, Chooses. What's it about? Who
do I shout? Is it a He? Is it a She? Who do I shout?
Who's about? Beggars, Chooses, Winners, Losers.
What are Newsers? Are they stories
about Fright and Delight?
Winners, Losers. Goodies, Baddies,
Happies, Sadies. Encourages, Abusers.
Newsers, Losers, Beggars, Chooses. Winners,
Losers in the Newsers. All of the Above.
All of the Below. Myths and Legends.
Winners, Losers, Beggars, Chooses.
In the Newsers. In the Newsers. In the Newsers.

SPOOKS AND ZOMBIES. NIGHTMARES AND DREAMS 18/08/2015 22:22

Spooks and Zombies on Pick TV. Here
I go again with the Poetry. Love these
things about Nightmares and Dreams.
Paranormal or Real? How do you Feel?
Unexplained or Unreal? How do you Feel?
Spooks and Zombies on Pick TV. Here I go
again with the Poetry. Love these things about
Nightmares and Dreams. Love these things
that bring Nightmares and Dreams. Love
these things about Nightmares and Dreams.
Love the Fear and the Joy that it brings.
Love the way they make the Mind Think.
Paranormal or Real? How do you Feel? You Decide.
Give your Mind a Ride.
Spooks and Zombies. Nightmares and
Dreams. Spooks and Zombies. Spooks
and Zombies. Spooks and Zombies.

I'M GONNA WONDER. IS THAT THUNDER ? 20/08/2015 0:10

I'm gonna Realize. I'm gonna Spiritualize.
I'm gonna Randomize. I'm gonna Minimize.
I'm gonna Visualize. I'm gonna Circumsize.
I'm gonna Customize. I'm gonna Wonder. I'm
gonna Wonder. I'm gonna Wonder. Is that
Thunder? Is that Thunder? Is that Thunder?
I'm Full of Hope. Stoned on Dope. Lamb Dinner
a Winner. Yummy in My Tummy. Mother's Away.
John and Bev's Retirement Doo Saturday. I'm
gonna Party. I'm gonna Play. I'm gonna have Fun
on Saturday. Maybe I get a Lay? I'm gonna Realize.
I'm gonna Spiritualize. I'm gonna Randomize. I'm
gonna Minimize. I'm gonna Visualize. I'm gonna
Circumsize. I'm gonna Customize. I'm gonna
Wonder. I'm gonna Wonder. I'm gonna Wonder.
Is that Thunder? Is that thunder? Is that Thunder?
It makes me Wonder? Goodbye
for Now. Wow, Wow, Wow.

STILL IMPORTIN'
20/08/2015 22:22

Still Importin' Music. It's Takin' Me Weeks.
Speakin' to Millie, Poppy and Lily-Rose.
All I got back was Meows and Squeaks. Cat
and Guinea Pigs, They Are. Finished till
Tuesday 6AM. Today is Thursday 10PM.
I still don't get What Happened Way back
When. If a Delorean made Me McFly Back
To Then. I'd do somethings Different and
somethings Again. I'd Never, Ever do some of
the things I did Way Back When, Again. Still
Importin' Music. It's Takin' Me Weeks.
Speakin' to Millie, Poppy and Lily-Rose. All
I got back was Meows and Squeaks. Cat and
Guinea Pigs, They Are. Still Importin' Music.
It's Takin' Me Weeks. Speakin' to
Millie, Poppy and Lily-Rose.
Gettin' back Meows and Squeaks.
Still Importin', Still Importin', Still
Importin', Still Importin', Still Importin',
Still Importin', Still Importin', Still Importin'
Music. Still Importin' My Tunes.

COLWICK LIFE
21/08/2015 16:00

Colwick Life. Colwick Strife. I've lived in
Colwick all my life. I love it here. I don't wanna
go anywhere. Colwick Life. Colwick Strife.
Colwick Life is pretty nice. Little Crime. Is the
44 On Time? Lots of Business. It's on a Major
Road Line. It's pretty quiet. Hardly a riot. Colwick
Life. Colwick Park is pretty great for a walk
or pork around. There's the Starting Gate The
Tobey Carvery too. Vale Club just over there.
The school with an Aeroplane just down there.
2 Off- Licence's, A Chemist, Community Centre,
Doctor's, Physio and Church. A Race Course.
A Dog Track. Look At That... Over There... I
Can't Believe My Stare... That Beautiful Building
Over There... It's Colwick Hall Standing Tall.
Colwick Life. Colwick Life. Colwick
Life. I love Colwick Life.

I·M IN LOVE 27/08/ MMXV 16:02

I'm in LOVE. I'm in LOVE. I'm in LOVE.
It's not a Bolt From Above. It's an
Old Flame to a New Flame.
I'm in LOVE. I'm in LOVE. I'm in LOVE.
I Hope it Will Be Better than the 1st Time. I Hope
it Will Be Better, but Almost the Same. We've
GROWN UP a bit. Made Decision's that were shit.
I'm in LOVE. I'm in LOVE. I'm in LOVE.
EMILY May have Her MUMMY and DADDY
Back? I'll See How it Goes? GOD ONLY KNOWS.
Maybe this is the Plan? Has the Re- Birth Began?
I Hope it Has. I Hope it Has. I Hope it Has.
I'm in LOVE. I'm in LOVE. I'm in LOVE.
Next 1st Date Monday. Bowling FunDay. I Feel
Joy At Last. Gonna Have a Blast. Hope This
Time it Does Last. Take it Steady and Not Fast.
I'm in LOVE. I'm in LOVE. I'm in LOVE.

CHEEZETUNEZ THRILL 30/08/ MMXV 15:29

I don't know if I'm in LOVE. Just skin up, bun
up, stone up and chill, to the CheezeTunez
Thrill. Good time of weekend. EMILY Thrill.
EMILY Grooving to DADDY's IPOD,
CheezeTunez Thrill. She's got Groovy Moves.
Maybe She'll Be a PopStar, Singing
DADDY's CheezeTunez Bluez?
Maybe doing Ballet and Dancing
CheezeTunez Lake?
Maybe a MovieStar, in CheezeTunez Filmz?
Skin up, bun up, stone up and chill,
to the CheezeTunez Thrill.
My Vibe is Changing. I Feel it in the Air. I wish
it be Amazing. Triple glazing. Big Ass House.
Big Ass Car. Big Ass Bucks. Big Ass Thrill.
Or Maybe the Same and Big ass Chill?
Nothing Doing. No CheezeTunez Thrill.
The Vibe is Changing. The Tide is Changing.
Maybe Amazing? Maybe Amazing?

Skin up, bun up, stone up and chill, to the
CheezeTunez Thrill. The CheezeTunez
Thrill. The CheezeTunez Thrill.
The End.

BOWLING FUNDAY, BANK HOLIDAY MONDAY 01/09/ MMXV 0:46

Had a Lovely Bowling FunDay, Bank Holiday Monday, with my Former Flame Anne. Emily got a STRIKE on her very 1st BOWL. In her very 1st game. On the 13th Lane! I won both games. Emily got 2nd and 3rd. Jo got 3rd and 2nd. Had a Lovely Bowling FunDay, Bank holiday Monday. We all got a STRIKE. Had a great day. What a delight. had a Lovely Bowling FunDay Bank Holiday Monday. We all had fun. Everybody won. It's about time. I don't know what's down the line. I'm ready for it now, wow, wow, wow. Time to walk the line. I'm ready for it this time. Had a Lovely Bowling Family FunDay, Bank Holiday Monday. Bowling FunDay, Bank Holiday Monday.

IT'S BEEN NON - STOP 17/09/2015 21:42

It's been Non-Stop for over a week. Trees Won Twice. Will I Ever get a Pay-Rise? Or Even a New Job? Please Help Me God. I Screwed it Up. I've been a Nob. Love and Hate. Burglary Spate. Garden gate.
Will I ever get Another Play-
Mate? Please Help me God.
I'm Down in the Dumps. I do lots of Trumps.
My Mind is Fuzzy. My Soul is Destroyed. My Heart is Broke. I'm a Normal Bloke. Life is a Maze. My Eyes are Glazed. Will My Spark Ever Re-Ablaze? I'm Under a Dome in a Lonely Home. My Aches are Back. My Soul is Sad. I Swing a lot from Happy and Sad, Normal and Glad, to Sane and Mad. I'm a Normal Bloke. I'm a Normal Bloke.
It's been Non-Stop. It's been Non-
Stop. It's been Non-Stop.

WHAT DID I WRITE T'OTHER NITE ?
19/09/2015 21:01

What did I write t'other nite? Was it good? Was it
shite? Will it bring pain? Will it bring gain? Will it
bring delite? Will it bring joy? Will it bring frite?
What did I write t'other nite?
Things that make sense. Things that go round
the bends. Things that bring friends. Things
that helped my mind mend. Things to love.
Things to hate. Things to like. Things to
take you out of site. What's it all about?
What did I write t'other nite?
Am I lost? Am I found? It's been a real roller-
coaster ride. I lost my mind. I found my
mind. I lost part of my heart and soul with
Madison and her Mum Jatinder! Was there
really a Demon in her? I think there was.
That's the reason because.
What did I write t'other nite? What
did I write t'other nite?
What did I write t'other nite?

MY LITTLE ·UN
20/09/2015 20:13

my little 'un. my little 'un. my little 'un.
when i see her, my boring life has some fun.
when i see her, i feel like i won. she's beautiful.
she's clever. she's bossy. she's silly. she's funny.
she costs me money. i love being her dad.
it's the best thing ever, in the never, never.
my little 'un. my little 'un. my little 'un.
my life's changed forever, in the never, never. when
i don't see her i'm sad. when i see her i'm glad. i
love being a dad. it's educational. it's emotional. it's
occupational. it's memorable. it's worrying. it's heart
breaking. it's people making. it's remembering. it's
amazing. being a dad. being a dad. being a dad.
it's happy and sad.
my little 'un. my little 'un. my little 'un.

I·M A BELIEVER
28/09/2015 22:27

I'm a believer. I've got the fever. I'm not a deceiver.
I'm a gud 'un. I'm a gud 'un.

I'm a believer. Where's the receiver? I'm lonely.
I'm homely. I've got gud bones. Body aching. Body
shaking. Body moaning. Body groaning. Body lost.
Body found. Body spinning. Spinning around.

Soul of a clown. Another frown. I'm a believer.
Where's the lever to push on? To have fun? Once it
begun, I needed a gun to end it all. In the fall. Red
leaves. **Yellow** leaves. Brown leaves. Orange leaves.
Green leaves. In the fall.

I'm a believer. I've got the fever. I'm not a deceiver.
Where's the reciever? I'm lonely. I'm homely.
I'm a gud 'un. I'm a gud 'un. I've got gud bones.
Body aching. Body shaking. Body moaning. Body
groaning. Body lost. Body found. In the ground.
In the ground. Body spinning. Spinning around.
I'm a believer. I'm a believer. I'm a believer.

MOON + STARS
01/10/2015 22:34

Where there's Moon + Stars. Wonderbra's + Cars.
Where there's Life + Death. Listerine Breath.
Is there Really Life on Mars? Sun + Water.
Beautiful Daughter. Moon + Stars. Bra's + Cars.
Music + Religion. Peace + War. Insomnia +
Snore. Peace Not War. Is this The End? What's
Around the Bend? Good + Bad. Happy + Sad.
Insane + Mad.
Where there's Moon + Stars. Bra's +
Cars. Slaughter + Redemption.
What Else is there to Question? Victory + Defeat.
Good + Bad. Happy + Sad. Poverty + Royalty.
Poetry + Apple Trees. Cure + Disease. World on
It's Knees. Moon + Stars is the Reason Because.
Tides + Landslides. Money + Greed. Fire +
Floods. Too Much Blood Over The Years. Your
Deepest Fears. Moon + Stars. Moon + Stars.
Moon + Stars. Moon + Stars. Etc...!

ON THE WINDS OF CHANGE 02/10/2015

Guinea Pigs + Hay Blowing away on the
winds of change. Bats + Rats. Mice + Cats.
Dogs + Hedgehogs Climbing the Logs.
Blowing away on the winds of change.
Fish + Fingers. Dead Ringers. Seals + Bears. Birds
+ Bees. Frogs + Toads. Monkeys + Junkies. Plants
+ Trees. Blowing away on the winds of change.
Humans + Aliens. Good + Bad. Music + Laughter.
Films + Dreams. Money + Greed. Farmers
Planting Seeds. Horses + Cars. Buildings +
Wasteland. Rivers + Lakes. Oceans + Seas.
Aeroplanes + Helicoptors. Army +
War. Poverty + Uncertainty.
Literature + Poetry. Welcome to Me.
Blowing away on the winds of change.
Spring + Summer. Autumn + Winter.
Going away on the winds of change.
On the winds of change. On the winds
of change. On the winds of change.

POETRY DAY
08/10/2015 19:30

Today is National Poetry Day. My body
aches. My mind complicates. I feel weak. I feel
rough. Does the collar match the cuffs? I'm
lost in space. I've got a stubbly face. I need
my hair cut. I'm still writing this book.
I feel like I've been given a right hook. The waters
ahead are full of muck. The futures uncertain.
Twitching curtains. The waters aren't clear.
They're full of fear. Loneliness is depressing me.
Sadness has taken over me. I need to climb a
tree and get some air. Who's that over there?
Today is National Poetry day. My body
aches. my bones shake. Will I ever learn
from the mistakes I make? My mind is
fuzzy. I'm feeling scuzzy. I'm feeling buzzy.
This is the end, my only friend, the end.
Poetry Day just went away. Poetry Day
has gone away. No more Poetry day.

THE THRILL HAS GONE
17/10/2015 21:41

The thrill has gone. What went wrong? The
thrill has gone. You done me wrong.
The thrill has gone. Life is dull. Life is uncool.
The thrill has gone. It's lonely. It's stonely.
The thrill has gone. Occasionally it's
happy. Occasionally it's whappy.
The thrill has gone. Occasionally
it's a good memory.
Occasionally it's a bad memory.
The thrill has gone. Lately it's been
lonely. Lately it's been moanly.
The thrill has gone. What went
wrong? You done me wrong.
The thrill has gone. The thrill has
gone. Life is dull. Life is uncool.
I've been a fool.
The thrill has gone. The thrill has
gone. Will it be number 1?
Will it become a song?
The thrill has gone. The thrill has
gone. The thrill has gone.

FAMILY HALLOWEEN
03/11/2015

Family Halloween went like a dream. Still no
Scream Queen. Life can be mean. Went for a New
Job at Bluekins. Yuletide Log. Trees are cack. Will
Dougie get the sack? Wish there was another
Clough and Taylor to be the trees saviour. Need
a different flavour. I need a Lottery favour.
Family Halloween went like a dream. I loved it
all. I did my 1st Pumpkin. It turned out great.
I've got a creative side. I need to decide what to
do. I'm off work with the Flu. I feel really cack.
I didn't get the New Job. Boss was a Nob. It went
to a fucking Polish Girl instead! We're being
Over-Ran by Foreigners Here! What can I do?
Is there a clue? It's foggy in here. It's foggy out
there. It's cold and damp. Walk the plank. I feel
like the Ships Mess! What do you suggest?
Family Halloween. Family Halloween.
Family Halloween.
It went like a dream.

DREAMS, SCREAMS, BODY CREAMS 16/11/2015 15:15

+ Dreams, Screams, Body Creams. Insect Bite.
Dark + Light. Let's have another site. Dreams
+ Nightmares. Frights + Delights. Shall we
go to bed tonight with, or without the light?
Dreams, Screams, Body Creams. Day + Night.
4 Seasons in 1 Day. Terror Hit! Terror Hit!
Holy Shit! Holy Shit! AK Shots! Many Got +.
Terror Hit! Terror Hit! What's it about? What's
this Religious Fight? Is it a Religious Rite?
Why these Screams? Why these Obscenes?
Why these Real Toxic dreams? Turning
Paris Life into Crime Scenes.
Blown to Bits! Holy Shit! For Who? But Why? Why
All the Cry? Religious Nuts is the Reason Because.
Un-Religious Nuts, More Like! BrainWash Time.
Do a Crime now you Brain's Washed away?.
Dreams, Screams, Body creams.
Religious Evil! Religious Evil! Religious Evil! +

IS IT THE END OF US ? 19/11/2015 14:41

Aeroplanes, Bombs, Tanks, Guns.
Terror, Despair, Hate, Pain.
Insane! Lots of Wrongs. What's Happened to
US? We've gone from Joy and Light, to Horror
and Night. With Greed and Disgust. Fright and
Not Delight. We've gone from Joy and Delight,
to Horror and Fright. What's Jihad Fight?
IS it the end of US? IS it the end
of US? IS it the end of US?
Helicoptors and Kalashnikovs. Blood and Guts.
Suicide Bombers. The Good are Dead. The
Bad are Dead. The Ugliness Messes with Your
Head. Are You Really Better Off Dead? Life
and Death. Take Your Last Breath. IS it Really
Worth It? I don't Think too Kindly of it. I
Think it's Wrong. No Ding-Dong. We've gone
from Joy and Light, to Horror and Fright.
IS it the end of US? IS it the end
of US? IS it the end of US?
IS it the end of US?

GIG NIGHTS
26/11/2015 22:41

Saw the Prodigy Tuesday Night. Great
Delight. What a Gig. Amazing Lights. Public
Enemy support were a lot better than Court.
Public Enemy support were better than I
thought. Gig wasn't as long as I hoped.
Which felt like a Con.
Enjoyed it though. Couldn't see it all, because
people in front were too tall. They Obscured my
View. This is True. Couldn't do owt about it though.
Thousands of Other People in the same Obscured
Woe. Bum's Bleeding Loads. I feel ill. Public
Enemy Joy. Prodigy Thrill. I Love Gig Nights.
Saw Happy Mondays Thursday Night. MadChester
Delight. Winachi Tribe support were better
than I thought. Winachi Tribe support were
better than the Stig. What a Gig. What a Gig
Night. Really Enjoyed it. It Changed my Sight.
Talking to Women gave me Great Delight.
Got Dentist Friday, to Remove my Tooth
decay. Happy Tuesday. Happy Thursday.
I Love Gig Nights. I Love Gig
Nights. I Love Gig Nights.
I Love My Gig Night Delights.

WEATHER'S BEEN COLD, WET AND GREY 28/11/2015 18:13

Trees Won today. Weather's been cold, wet and grey. Santa's only 4 weeks away. Trees Won today. Weather's been cold, wet and grey. Saw my Emily today, so it was an even happier and better day. When I took her back and got home, it became a really wet day. Window Cleaner's came. That'll explain the rain today. Everytime they come, it rains that day. Even on a Sunny Day. Window Cleaners come and there's usually some sort of rain that day. I Joke you Not. Trees Won today. Weather's been cold, wet and grey. It's been raining Cat's, dog's, Men and Frog's. Trees Won today. Weather's been cold, wet and grey. It's been a very happy day. Santa's only 4 weeks away. Weather's been cold, wet and grey. Weather's been cold, wet and grey. Weather's been bad today.

MILLIEKIN BLUES
28/11/2015 20:15

I'm lying down Thinking of the Milliekin Blues.
Are the Doors of Perception going to Un-Close?
I'm lying down Thinking about the Milliekin Blues.
I'm listening to the CheezeTunes Blues. My mind is
calm. I'm gonna In-Fuse. Tummy's Grumbling. I've
got a Pizza Cooking. Footy Night Saturday Night.
I can watch it tonight with Delight and No Fright.
I'm lying down Thinking of the Milliekin Blues.
I'm sitting here Writing the Milliekin Blues.
Getting some help from the CheezeTunes Blues.
Music is the Best thing in the World. I Love
Music. I Love my CheezeTunes Pearls.
I Wish Music Could Heal the World?
I'm lying down Thinking of the Milliekin Blues.
I'm sitting here Writing the Milliekin Blues.
The Milliekin Blues. The Milliekin
Blues. The Milliekin Blues.

STRONGBOWADE
28/11/2015 20:53

Strongbowade is what I made, with Jif **Lemon** in the glass. Then it made my tabs laugh. It really tastes nice. Drink it with watering eyes. Strongbowade is what I made.

IN THE LAND OF NEVER
29/11/2015 15:12

In the Land of Never, I started to Quiver.
I started to shiver. I started to Fear.
I started to Scream. Enter Night. Exit Light.
In the Land of Never. It's a Scary Place. It's
a Creepy Place. It's a Frightening Place. It's
Never a Happy Place. It's a Lonely Place. It's
an UN- Holy Place. It's a Soul-Less Place.
In the Land of Never. You Never want
to remember the Land of never.
I started to Quiver. I started to Shiver. I started to
fear. I started to Scream. Enter Night. Exit Light.
In the Land of Never. In the Land of
Never. In the Land of never.

THE WIND IS HOWLING. THE WIND IS GROWLING 29/11/2015 18:51

The wind is howling. the wind is growling.
Bringing the rain. Bringing the pain. Fences
rattling. Trees up-rooting. Branches breaking.
Leaves are blowing in the wind.
The wind is howling. The wind is
growling. Bringing the rain.
Blowing around the pain.
The wind is howling. The wind is growling.
The wind is gusting. The wind is blustery.
The wind is blowing away the best of me. The
wind is blowing away the rest of me. The wind
is up-rooting trees. Blowing away dreams.
Leaves are blowing in the wind.
The wind is howling. The wind is growling.
Bringing the rain. Blowing cobwebs out of your
brain. Blowing fences over. Damaging roofs.

Blowing away the lies. Blowing away
the truths. Up-rooting trees.
Rattling fences. Damaging roofs.
The wind is howling. The wind is growling.
Bringing the rain. Bringing the pain. The wind is
howling. The wind is growling. Blowing to the end.

THE STARS ARE OUT 04/12/2105 0:36

The Stars are out. What's Life about? It's
full of See-Saws and Uproars. Opening,
Closing and Revolving Doors. It's full of Yes's
and No's, Camel Toes. It's full of moments
of, Should I stay, or Should I go's.
The Stars are out. What's Life about? It's full of
Highs and Lows. It's full of, Should I stay, or Should
I go's. It's full of Yes's and No's, Camel Toes.
The Stars are out. Who knows what Life's about?
Fakers and Fraudsters. Sons and Daughters.
Pirates and Treasure. Pain and Pleasure.
Love and War, in the Revolving Door.
The stars are out. What's Life about?
See-Saws and Uproars.
Opening and Closing Doors.
The Stars are out. The Stars are
out. The Stars are out.
What's Life about?

BOO HOO HOO
04/12/2015 22:27

I hurt my left wrist today. I did it bending
pizza cartons. Been bending for weeks. Been
starting to get some tweaks, here and there.
Twisted my ankle too.
Boo Hoo Hoo. Boo Hoo Hoo. Boo Hoo Hoo.
My left wrist went crack. The pain was
So bad. The pain was So bad.
Saw 1st Aider and he reported and checked
it for me. He did me a favour. It's throbbing
now. I can move it and use it, but it hurts
quite a bit. I don't want to abuse it. I hurt my
left wrist today. What a day. It happened at
the end of the week. The pain was unique.
Boo Hoo Hoo. Boo Hoo Hoo. Boo Hoo Hoo.
It's throbbing lots. It won't be forgot. Don't want
the crack, to become bad. Take me to the Hospital.
Don't think it's broke. I'm just an Unlucky bloke.
Boo Hoo Hoo. Boo Hoo Hoo. Boo Hoo Hoo.
Boo Hoo Hoo. Boo Hoo Hoo. Boo Who How?

ICE ROAD TRUCKIN'
08/12/2015 0:36

Ice Road Truckin'. Snow Chains
strugglin'. Arctic Vortex comin'.
Better start Truckin'. Will they get Back? Will
they get the Sack? Ice Road Truckin'. Snow Chains
strugglin'. Arctic Vortex comin'. Snow comin' down,
Disappearin' the Ground. Where's the Road Gone?
This is Not fun!
Who's the Best? What about the Rest?
Ice Road Truckin'. Snow Chains strugglin'.
Snow comin' down, Disappearin' the Ground.
Where's the Road Gone? Arctic Vortex
comin'. Who Will Survive? Will they Be
Alive? Take it Steady. Always Be Ready.
Crossin' the Lake. Will the Ice Break?
Is it Survival? Is it Fate? Who Will be
the Best? Who Will be the Great? Who
Will be Worst? Who Will Break?
Ice Road Truckin', Crossin' the Lake. Will The
Ice Break? Ice Road Truckin. Ice Road Truckin',
Crossin' the Lake. Is This the Time, When the Ice
Breaks? Ice Road Truckin'. Ice Road Survivin'.

+ LEE HARVEY +
08/12/2015 12:01

+++ My mate Lee Harvey Passed Away, the other
day. Something burst. The scenario that was worst.
He was only 38. That's no age, these days. Did he
know, before he went through the Pearly gate's?
Will we never know?
He wasn't close to me. Every now and
then, I'd catch up with him. He had a heart
of gold. He was misunderstood. I sort of
understood him. We were on the same
equilibrium. He understood me, thankfully.
He was 1 of the good 1's, who's early roots, could
easily turn him into a bad 1. They didn't though.
He was lonely, like me. Now he's been freed, from
all the trouble and toil. Nice knowing you Lee.
Thankyou for the memories.
Say hello to God for me. Adios Amigo. R.I.P. +++

SUNNY WEDNESDAY
09/12/2015 12:09

I saw the Charlatans last night. More MadChester
delight. My favourite and last gig of the
year. Got very drunk. Drank way too much
beer. When I got home, I was sick all night
long. Where did all the sick come from?
Went to the Hospital Monday. The Nurse checked
me. She said I've bruised and torn the ligaments.
in my left wrist slightly. It still hurts to lift
things and twist my left wrist. I feel hungover
today. At least it's a Sunny Wednesday.
I want a new job. I'm fed up of the greedy
Bluekins nobs. All the silly little rules. It's
worse than being at school. Those shady,
greedy, silly, Bluekins fools. Working at
Bluekins has brought me nowt, but bad luck.
Immigrants getting 3 outta 4 new jobs
in England, has left me stuck.
We need to close the borders, to
bring back the good luck.
It's a hungover and Sunny Wednesday today.

NUMBERS, NUMBERS
10/12/2015 16:34

Numbers, Numbers. What are these Numbers
in my head? What do they mean? Is it the
beginning of the dream, coming to life?
Is it money? Is it a wife?
Numbers, Numbers. What are
these Numbers in my head?
Are they money? Are they honey? What a trip.
What a dream. What was it about? The scenes are
hard to work out. It scared me. It excited me. It
made me cry. It was like a 2nd sight, a 6th sense. A lot
of memories. So much stuff. I could write a book.
Numbers, Numbers. What are these Numbers
in my head? Was it a premonition? Was it a
vision? Was it a mission? Was it intuition?
Numbers, Numbers. What are
these Numbers in my head?
Is it a book, that has to be wrote and read?
Number, Numbers. Come and join us.
Numbers, Numbers. Come and join us.

IT'S DARK AND GLOOMY. IS ANYBODY COMING FOR ME? 10/12/2015 17:01

I walked into Steph the Nurse today. Very
pretty. She checked my left wrist again. It was
the same news as the 1st Nurse. Take it easy.
Take it steady and in a few weeks time,
my wrist will be ready. Can't
get hold of my Doctor yet, to get
a note, to prove the truth.
Fell out with my boss today. He put me on
the same job, that hurt my wrist, back then!
I went mad at him. I'm not dim. Got told
off by our other boss. I was very mad. I told
him what happened at work, back then. I
didn't lose my rag. It was an emotional 1.
Hope the healing's begun. I feel strange
again. I'm gonna count to

10. I'm highly strung. Has the end begun?
I'm lost in space. The clock is ticking.
What's it about? What was I thinking?
It's dark and gloomy. Is anybody coming for me?
It's dark and gloomy. Is anybody coming for me?
It's dark and gloomy. Is anybody coming for me?

MY LITTLE RED BOOK 10/12/2015 20:00

So I've got to the end of *my little red book*, my friends. I enjoyed writing it. I wrote it in parts: *1* and *2*. I enjoyed reading it. I enjoyed the mending, minding bits. It ended with a Real Death, just like *my little blue book*.
+ GOD BLESS YOU LEE +. Thankyou for showing me my family. Nice meeting you Addison, Dad, Uncles + Aunties, Grandmas + Grandads. Thankyou for the advice. It gave me a Happy, Heavenly, Mind Ride. Nice meeting you all again. It Truly Was Heaven Sent.
So I've got to the end of *my little red, parts: 1 + 2*. Plus the original *little blue* too. I may have mended myself? We'll soon be surrounded by Christmas Elfs. Presents to un-wrap. Crackers to snap. This is the end of *my little red book*, my friends. *Part 2* here, now ends.

THIS IS THE END OF MY LITTLE
RED BOOK : Part 2 …
ALSO AVAILABLE :
MY LITTLE RED BOOK : Part 1 (2014 - 2015)
MY LITTLE BLUE BOOK (2006 - 2014)
By The C heezeBoy

M . I . M . CheezeBooks Ltd.

www.ingramcontent.com/pod-product-compliance
Lightning Source LLC
Chambersburg PA
CBHW020920140626
46545CB00015B/1013